# 24 Blocks
## You Never Dreamed You Could Paper Piece

## Introduction

Have you ever seen a block that you would love to sew, but don't want to cut dozens of diamond shapes or do inset or curved piecing? So, you go back to making Nine Patch or Log Cabin or just something more "comfortable."

*24 Blocks You Never Dreamed You Could Paper Piece*, allows you to make complicated blocks without cutting shapes ahead of time and you will not have to do any inset piecing and you can make blocks with curves by sewing straight lines. On top of that, your points will be pointy, not flat.

Some of the blocks in this book are simple to do, so you may want to start out making those. But, some are more complex and have many pieces. Just take your time, follow the piecing diagram and refer to the color block pattern in the book. You will then end up with beautiful blocks that "you never dreamed you could paper piece."

Editorial: Bobbie Matela, Linda Causee, and Christina Wilson
Technical Artist: Chad Summers
Production: Ronda Bechinski

Thank you to the following companies who generously supplied products for our blocks:

Bernina® of America: Artista 180 sewing machine

Güterman: 100% cotton sewing thread

Bali Fabrics, Inc: Princess Mirah Design batik

Pictured blocks were made by Linda Causee, Robin Radovich and Kathy Wesley.

**American School of Needlework™**
excellence in instruction

1455 Linda Vista Drive
San Marcos, CA 92069
www.ASNpub.com
©2003 American School of Needlework Inc.

The full line of ASN products is carried by Annie's Attic catalog.
**TOLL FREE ORDER LINE** or to request a free catalog (800) 582-6643
visit www.AnniesAttic.com
**Customer Service** (800) 282-6643, **Fax** (800) 882-6643

ISBN: 1-59012-066-3
Printed in U.S.A.
456789

# General Directions

## About the Patterns

All of the blocks in this book are 10" finished. The full-color patterns have more than one section that must be foundation-pieced individually, and then sewn together. For the blocks made up of four equal sections, we have included only one section that will need to be traced four times to complete the block, **Fig 1**.

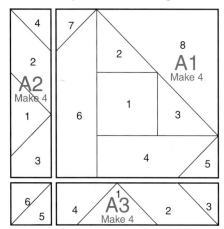

**Fig 1**

For the blocks made up of different sections (labeled A, B, C, etc.), we have included one of each section explaining how many of each you will have to sew, **Fig 2**. Each section may contain smaller sections that will need to be pieced individually first. Bold lines that are

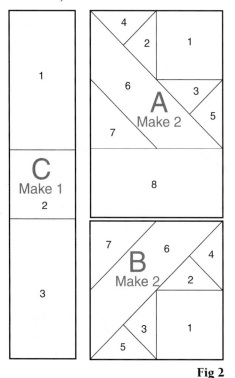

**Fig 2**

also the cutting lines indicate these sections. A piecing diagram is included with each block pattern showing the piecing order of the sections.

Also included with each block pattern is a photograph showing the completed block. Note the finished blocks are mirror images of the original patterns, **Fig 3**. This means that some of the colors on the finished blocks could be in opposite places from colors on pattern. Note the placement of the green and orange in center of Carpenter's Wheel in **Fig 3**.

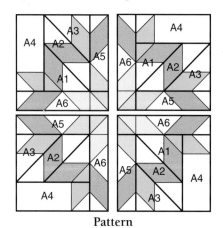

**Pattern**

**Finished Block**

**Fig 3**

## The Foundation Piecing Method

### Foundation Material

Before you start sewing, you need to decide the type of foundation on which to piece your blocks. There are several options. Paper is a popular choice for machine piecing because it is readily available and inexpensive. Copier paper works well, but newsprint found in office supply stores is much easier to handle

since it is not as stiff. The paper is removed after the blocks are completely sewn.

Another alternative for foundation piecing is muslin or cotton fabric that is light-colored and lightweight for easy tracing. The fabric will add another layer that you will have to quilt through, but that is only a consideration if you are going to hand-quilt. Also, if you use a fabric foundation, you will be able to hand-piece your blocks if that is your desire.

A third option for foundation material is Tear Away® or Fun-dational™ translucent non-woven material. Like muslin, it is light enough to see through for tracing, but like paper, it can be easily removed before quilting.

A new type of "disappearing" foundation material by W. H. Collins is called WashAway™ foundation paper. After sewing, place block in water and the foundation dissolves in ten seconds.

## Preparing the Foundation

### Tracing the Block

Trace the block pattern carefully onto your chosen foundation material. Use a ruler and a fine-point permanent marker or fine-line mechanical pencil to make straight lines; be sure to include all numbers and letters for multiple sections. Repeat for the number of blocks needed for your quilt.

### Transferring the Block

The block pattern can also be transferred onto foundation material, but to do this involves an additional step if you want your block to look like the photographed block. First, trace the block pattern onto tracing paper. Flop the paper so that the design is "backwards" and trace again onto plain paper using a transfer pen or pencil, **Fig 4**.

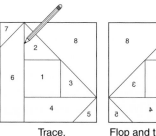

Trace.     Flop and trace again.

**Fig 4**

Then, following manufacturers directions, iron transferred design onto foundation material. If these steps are not followed, your finished block will be a mirror image of the finished block shown, **Fig 5**.

Finished Block        Mirror Image

**Fig 5**

## Fabric

We recommend using 100-percent cotton fabric for piecing. By using cotton rather than cotton/polyester blends, the pieces will not slip as easily and they will respond better to finger pressing.

Prewashing fabric is not necessary, but it is advisable to test your fabric to make certain that the fabric is colorfast (don't trust manufacturers' labels). Place a 2"-wide strip (cut crosswise) of fabric into a bowl of extremely hot water; if the water changes color, the fabric is bleeding and it will be necessary to wash that fabric until all of the excess dye has washed out. Repeat for all fabrics that will be used for your quilt. Fabrics that continue to bleed after they have been washed several times should be eliminated.

To test for shrinkage, take each saturated strip (used above in the colorfast test) and iron it dry with a hot iron. When the strip is completely dry, measure and compare it to your original 2" measurements. If all of your strips shrink about the same amount, then you really have no problem. When you wash your quilt, you may achieve the puckered look of an antique quilt. If you do not want this look, you will have to wash and dry all fabric before beginning so that shrinkage is no longer an issue. If any of your test strips are shrinking more than the others, these fabrics will need to be prewashed and dried, or discarded.

## Cutting the Fabric

One of biggest advantages to foundation piecing is that you do not have to cut exact pieces for every block. This is especially important for smaller blocks or blocks with many small pieces. It is much easier to handle a small section or strip of

fabric than it is to handle a triangle where the finished size of the sides is 1/4".

The main consideration for using fabric pieces for a particular space is that the fabric must be at least 1/4" larger on all sides than the space it is to cover. Squares and strips are easy to figure, but triangle shapes can be a little tricky to piece. Use generous-sized fabric pieces and be careful when positioning the pieces onto the foundation. You do waste some fabric this way, but the time it saves in cutting will be worth it in the end.

*Hint: Measure the width of a particular space on your pattern; add 1/2" and cut strips that width, **Fig 6**. You will save time since you won't have to trim each seam allowance as you go.*

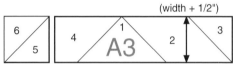

**Fig 6**

## How to Make a Foundation-Pieced Block

**1.** Prepare foundations as described on the previous page in Preparing the Foundation, making the number of each section as shown on the pattern. Cut foundations apart along the bold lines to separate pattern into smaller sections, **Fig 7**.

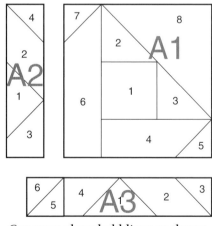

**Cut apart along bold lines as shown.**

**Fig 7**

**2.** Starting with section A1, turn foundation section with unmarked side facing you and position piece 1 right side up over the space marked "1" on the foundation. Hold foundation up to a light source to make sure that fabric overlaps at least 1/4" on all sides of space 1, **Fig 8**. Pin or use a glue stick to hold fabric in place.

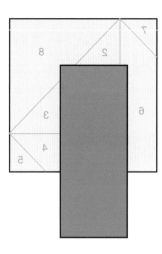

**Fig 8**

*Hint: Use only a small dab of a fresh glue stick to hold fabric in place.*

**3.** Turn foundation over. With marked side of foundation facing you, fold foundation forward along line between space 1 and 2 and trim fabric about 1/4" from fold if needed, **Fig 9**.

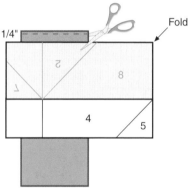

**Fig 9**

**4.** Place fabric piece 2 right sides together with piece 1; edge of fabric 2 should be even with just-trimmed edge of fabric 1, **Fig 10**.

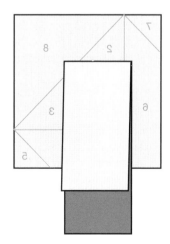

**Fig 10**

Double check to see if fabric piece chosen will cover space 2 completely by folding over along line between space 1 and 2, **Fig 11**.

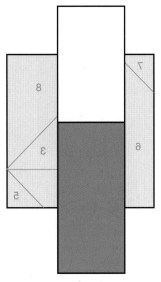

**Fig 11**

**5.** With marked side of foundation facing you, place on sewing machine, holding fabric pieces together. Sew along line between spaces 1 and 2 using a very small stitch (18 to 20 stitches per inch), **Fig 12**. Begin and end sewing two to three stitches beyond line. You do not need to backstitch.

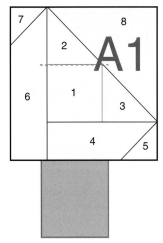

**Fig 12**

*Hint: Sewing with a very tiny stitch will allow for easier paper removal later. If paper falls apart after stitching, your stitch length is too small and you will need to lengthen the stitch slightly.*

**6.** Turn foundation over. Open piece 2 and finger-press seam, **Fig 13**. Use a pin or dab of glue stick to hold piece in place if necessary. *Hint: If using strips, trim extra length being sure to leave enough to cover entire area plus seam allowance.*

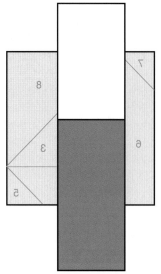

**Fig 13**

**7.** Turn foundation with marked side of foundation facing you; fold foundation forward along line between spaces 1 and 3 and trim ¹/₄" from fold if necessary, **Fig 14**. *Note: If you have used a pre-measured strip as described in Cutting the Fabric, you will not need to do this step.*

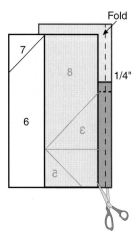

**Fig 14**

**8.** Place fabric 3 right side down, even with just-trimmed edge, **Fig 15**.

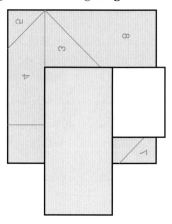

**Fig 15**

**9.** Turn foundation to marked side and sew along line between spaces 1 and 3; begin and end sewing two to three stitches beyond line, **Fig 16**.

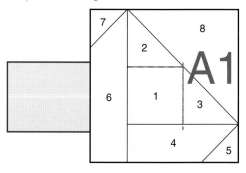

**Fig 16**

**10.** Turn foundation over, open piece 3 and finger-press seam. Glue or pin in place, **Fig 17**.

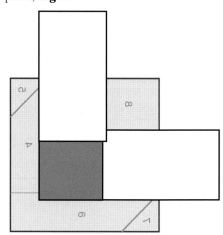

**Fig 17**

**11.** Turn foundation with marked side facing you. Fold foundation forward along line between spaces 1, 3 and 4; trim to about ¼" from fold, **Fig 18**.

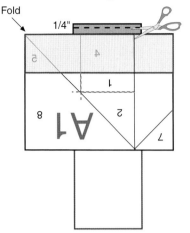

**Fig 18**

*Hint: If using a paper foundation, carefully pull paper away from stitching for easier trimming. If using a fabric foundation, fold it forward as far as it will go and trim.*

**12.** Place fabric 4 right side down, even with just-trimmed edge. With marked side of foundation facing you, sew along line between spaces 1, 3 and 4, **Fig 19**.

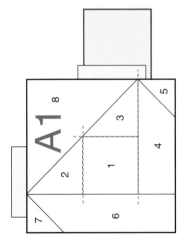

**Fig 19**

**13.** Continue trimming and sewing pieces in numerical order until section is complete, **Fig 20**. Make sure pieces along the outer edge are large enough to allow for the ¼" seam allowance.

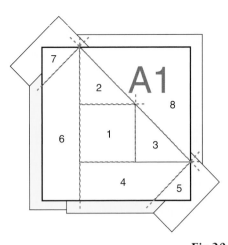

**Fig 20**

**14.** Press, then trim fabric ¼" from outside line of foundation to complete section, **Fig 21**.

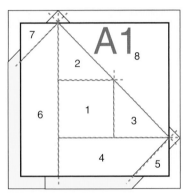

**Fig 21**

**15.** Complete remaining sections of block in same manner, **Fig 22**.

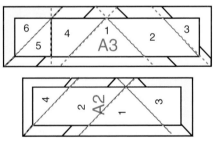

**Fig 22**

**16.** To sew sections, place right sides together; push a pin through corner of top section going through to corner of bottom section. Check to be sure pin goes through both corners and is perpendicular (going straight up) to section, **Fig 23**. If not, pin again until corners match.

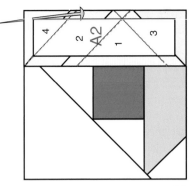

**Fig 23**

Repeat at opposite end of seam line to match corners. It is also a good idea to pin the intersections of seams that should line up between the two sections, **Fig 24**.

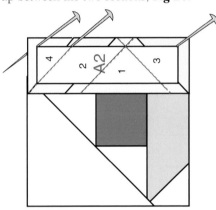

**Fig 24**

*Hint: If desired, baste sections together by hand or machine. Check sections again; if everything matches up, sew together with regular stitches. Basting takes a little time, but the extra effort will be worth it in the end.*

**17.** Once pieces are lined up correctly, sew along edge of foundation using a regular stitch length, **Fig 25**.

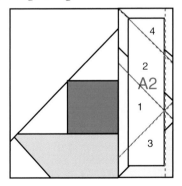

**Fig 25**

**18.** Sew remaining sections together, referring to the order in the piecing diagram with each pattern.

*Hint: Do not remove paper yet. It is better to remove paper after blocks have been sewn together. Since grain line was not considered in piecing, outer edges may be on the bias and, therefore, stretchy. Keeping paper in place until after sewing will prevent the blocks from becoming distorted. Stay stitching along outer edge of block,* **Fig 26,** *will also help keep fabric from stretching out of shape.*

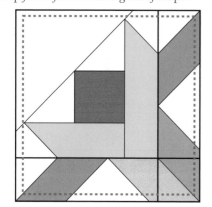

**Fig 26**

## Highlights and Hints for Foundation Piecing

• Begin and end sewing at least two to three stitches beyond line you are sewing on, **Fig 27.**

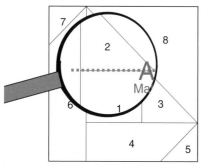

**Fig 27**

• Don't worry if your stitching goes through a whole space and into another space, **Fig 28;** it will not interfere with adding subsequent pieces.

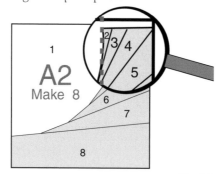

**Fig 28**

• Finger-press or press with an iron after every seam. The little wooden "irons" found in quilt shops or catalogs work great.

• Use a short stitch, around 20 stitches per inch.

• Trim seam allowances to $1/8$" to $1/4$" (or smaller if necessary).

• Don't worry too much about grain line. Sewing to a foundation stabilizes the fabric and will prevent it from getting out of shape.

• When sewing spaces with points, it is easier to start sewing from the wide end towards the point, **Fig 29.**

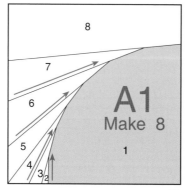

**Fig 29**

• Directional prints are not recommended unless they are used only once in a block or are placed where they can be used easily in a consistent manner, **Fig 30.**

**Like this**

**Fig 30**

If directional prints are placed randomly, the effect in the finished block may be undesirable, **Fig 31.**

**Not like this**

**Fig 31**

## Making A Quilt

The following layouts show what some of the blocks will look like when put together or combined with another block. If you would like to make these quilts, we have included the yardage requirements and suggested cutting to make piecing easier.

### Layout 1 – Oh Susannah

Approximate Size: 51" x 51"
Block Used: 16 Oh Susannah Blocks
(page 25)

### Materials
*Oh Susannah Blocks*
• 1 yd fabric 1
• $5/8$ yd fabric 2
• $1/2$ yd fabric 3
• $1/2$ yd fabric 4

*Finishing*
• $3/8$ yd border 1 fabric
• $7/8$ yd border 2 fabric
• $1/2$ yd binding fabric
• 3 yds backing fabric

### Suggested Cutting
*Oh Susannah Blocks*
• Six $3/4$" strips, fabric 1
• Three $2^3/4$" strips, fabric 1
• Nine $2^1/4$" strips, fabric 2
• Six $2^1/4$" strips, fabric 3
• Five $2^3/4$" strips, fabric 4

*Finishing*
• Five 2" strips, border 1 fabric
• Six $4^1/2$" strips, border 2 fabric
• Six $2^1/2$" strips, binding fabric

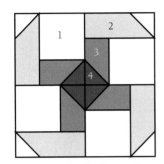

**Oh Susannah Block – Fabrics**

## Layout 2 – Desert Rose

Approximate Size: 55" x 55"
Block Used: 16 Desert Rose
Blocks (page 16)

### Materials

*Desert Rose Blocks*
- $1^{1}/2$ yds fabric 1
- $^{1}/4$ yd fabric 2
- $^{5}/8$ yd fabric 3
- $^{5}/8$ yd fabric 4
- $^{1}/2$ yd fabric 5
- $^{1}/2$ yd fabric 6

*Finishing*
- $^{1}/4$ yd border 1 fabric
- $^{1}/2$ yd border 2 fabric
- $^{7}/8$ yd border 3 fabric
- $^{1}/2$ yd binding fabric
- $3^{1}/4$ yds backing fabric

### Suggested Cutting

***Note:*** *Cut fabric into strips, then cut strips as you piece referring to How to Make a Foundation-Pieced Block, pages 3 to 5.*

*Desert Rose Blocks*
- Four 4" strips, fabric 1
- Seven 2" strips, fabric 1
- Eight $2^{1}/2$" strips, fabric 1
- Four 2" strips, fabric 2
- 14 – $1^{1}/2$" strips, fabric 3
- 12 - $1^{1}/2$" strips, fabric 4

- Four 2" strips, fabric 5
- Two $1^{1}/2$" strips, fabric 5
- Four 2" strips, fabric 6
- Two $1^{1}/2$" strips, fabric 6

*Finishing*
- Five $1^{1}/2$" strips, border 1 fabric

- Five 3" strips, border 2 fabric
- Six $4^{1}/2$" strips, border 3 fabric
- Six $2^{1}/2$" strips, binding fabric

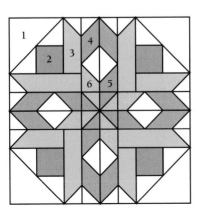

**Desert Rose Block – Fabrics**

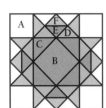

**Twinkling Star Block – Fabrics**

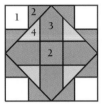

**Stars and Crosses Block – Fabrics**

## Layout 3 – Stars and Crosses

Approximate Size: 66" x 76"
Blocks Used: 15 Twinkling Star Blocks (page 34) and 15 Cross Within a Cross Blocks (page 32)

### Materials

*Cross Within a Cross Blocks*
- $1/2$ yd fabric 1
- $3/4$ yd fabric 2
- $5/8$ yd fabric 3
- $3/8$ yd fabric 4

*Twinkling Star Blocks*
- $7/8$ yd fabric A
- $1/4$ yd fabric B
- $3/8$ yd fabric C
- $1/2$ yd fabric D
- $3/8$ yd fabric E
- $5/8$ yd fabric F

*Finishing*
- $5/8$ yd border 1
- $11/4$ yds border 2
- $1/2$ yd binding
- $33/4$ yds backing

### Suggested Cutting

*Note: Cut fabric into strips, then cut strips as you piece referring to How to Make a Foundation-Pieced Block, pages 3 to 5.*

*Cross Within a Cross Blocks*
- Five 3" strips, fabric 1

- Seven $31/2$" strips, fabric 2
- Seven 3" strips, fabric 3
- Three $31/2$" strips, fabric 4

*Twinkling Star Blocks*
- Nine 3" strips, fabric A
- Two $41/2$" strips, fabric B
- Three $31/2$" strips, fabric C
- Five 3" strips, fabric D
- Three 3" strips, fabric E
- Seven 3" strips, fabric F

*Finishing*
- Six 3" strips, border 1 fabric
- Seven 6" strips, border 2 fabric
- Seven $21/2$" strips, binding fabric

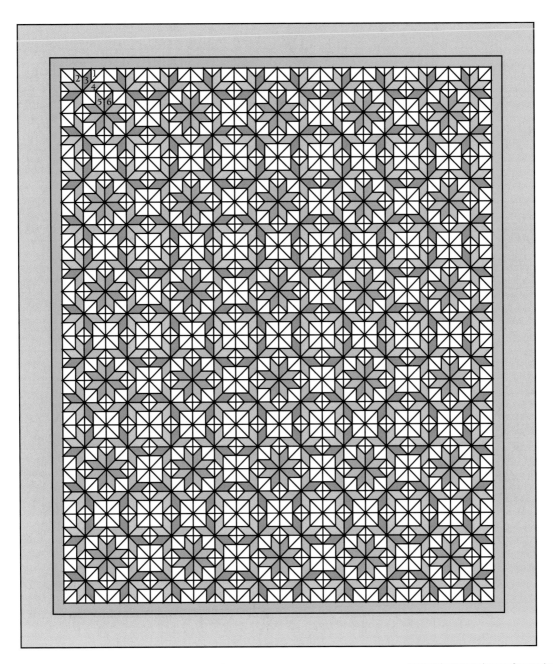

## Layout 4 – Snow Crystals

Approximate Size: 60" x 70"
Block Used: 30 Snow Crystals Blocks
(page 21)

### Materials
*Snow Crystals Blocks*
- 3¹/₂ yds fabric 1
- ⁷/₈ yd fabric 2
- ⁷/₈ yd fabric 3
- ⁷/₈ yd fabric 4
- ¹/₂ yd fabric 5
- ¹/₂ fabric 6

*Finishing*
- ¹/₂ yd border 1
- ⁷/₈ yd border 2
- ⁵/₈ yd binding
- 3¹/₂ yds backing

### Suggested Cutting
*Note: Cut fabric into strips, then cut strips as you piece referring to How to Make a Foundation-Pieced Block, pages 3 to 5.*

*Snow Crystals Blocks*
- 30 – 2¹/₂" strips, fabric 1
- 24 – 2" strips, fabric 1
- 18 – 1¹/₂" strips, fabric 2
- 18 – 1¹/₂" strips, fabric 3
- 18 – 1¹/₂" strips, fabric 4
- Nine 1¹/₂" strips, fabric 5
- Nine 1¹/₂" strips, fabric 6

*Finishing*
- Six 2" strips, border 1 fabric
- Seven 4" strips, border 2 fabric
- Seven 2¹/₂" strips, binding

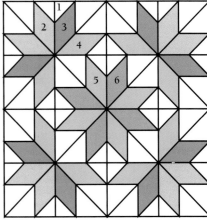

**Snow Crystals Block – Fabrics**

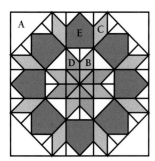

**Star of Bethlehem
Block – Fabrics**

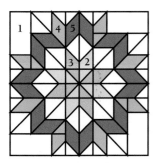

**Carpenter's Wheel
Block – Fabrics**

## Layout 5 – Carpenter's Star

Approximate Size: 82" x 102"
Blocks Used: 31 Carpenter's Wheel Blocks
(page 17) and 32 Star of Bethlehem Blocks
(page 28)

### Materials

*Carpenter's Wheel Blocks*
- $3^1/4$ yds fabric 1
- 1 yd fabric 2
- $1/2$ yd fabric 3
- 1 yd fabric 4
- 2 yds fabric 5

*Star of Bethlehem Blocks*
- 3 yds fabric A
- $3/4$ yd fabric B
- $1^1/8$ yds fabric C
- $3/4$ yd fabric D
- 2 yds fabric E

*Finishing*
- $5/8$ yds border 1
- $1^1/2$ yds border 2
- $3/4$ yd binding
- $7^1/8$ yds backing

### Suggested Cutting

*Note: Cut fabric into strips, then cut strips
as you piece referring to How to Make a
Foundation-Pieced Block, pages 3 to 5.*

*Carpenter's Wheel Blocks*
- 24 – 2" strips fabric 1
- 24 – $2^1/2$" strips, fabric 1
- 22 – $1^1/2$" strips, fabric 2
- 12 – $1^1/2$"strips, fabric 3

- 22 – $1^1/2$" strips, fabric 4
- 44 – $1^1/2$" strips, fabric 5

*Star of Bethlehem Blocks*
- Seven 4" strips, fabric A
- 32 – 2" strips, fabric A
- Four $2^1/2$" strips, fabric A
- Five 2" strips, fabric B
- Nine $1^1/2$" strips, fabric B
- 23 - $1^1/2$" strips, fabric C
- Nine $1^1/2$" strips, fabric D
- Five 2" strips, fabric D
- 23 – 3" strips, fabric E

*Finishing*
- Nine 2" strips, border 1 fabric
- Ten 5" strips, border 2 fabric
- Ten $2^1/2$" strips, binding fabric

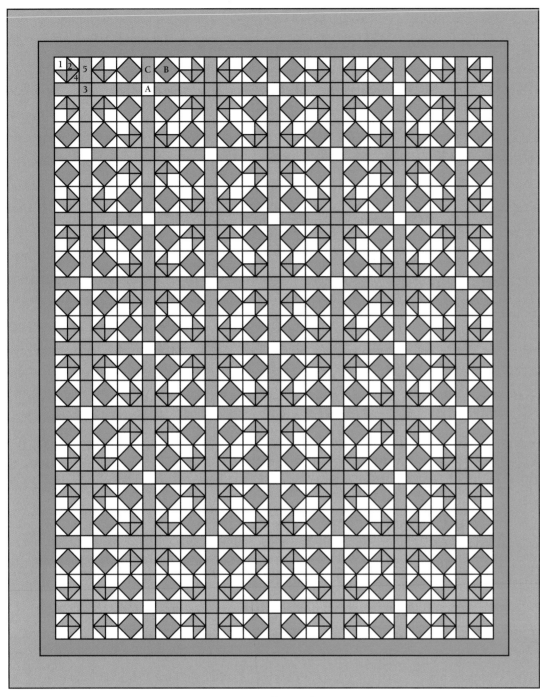

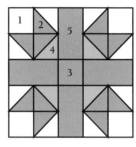

**Heavenly Problems
Block – Fabrics**

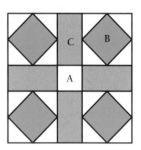

**Garden of Eden
Block – Fabrics**

## Layout 6 – Heavenly Garden

Approximate Size: 85" x 105"
Blocks Used: 32 Heavenly Problems Blocks
(page 42) and 31 Garden of Eden Blocks
(page 40)

### Materials:
*Heavenly Problems Blocks*
- $1^5/8$ yd fabric 1
- $1^5/8$ yd fabric 2
- $5/8$ yd fabric 3
- $5/8$ yd fabric 4
- $1^1/2$ yd fabric 5

*Garden of Eden Blocks*
- 2 yds fabric A
- $1^7/8$ yds fabric B
- $1^1/8$ yds fabric C

*Finishing*
- $7/8$ yd border 1 fabric
- $1^5/8$ yds border 2 fabric
- $3/4$ yd binding fabric
- $7^1/2$ yds backing fabric

### Suggested Cutting
*Note: Cut fabric into strips, then cut strips
as you piece referring to How to Make a
Foundation-Pieced Block, pages 3 to 5.*

*Heavenly Problems Blocks*
- Eight $2^1/2$" strips, fabric 1
- Twelve 3" strips, fabric 1

- Twelve 3" strips, fabric 2
- Six 3" strips, fabric 3
- Two $2^1/2$" strips, fabric 3
- Six 3" strips, fabric 4
- 15 – $2^1/2$" strips, fabric 5

*Garden of Eden Blocks*
- Two $2^1/2$" strips, fabric A
- 22 – $3^1/8$" strips, fabric A
- 14 – $4^1/2$" strips, fabric B
- 14 – $2^1/2$" strips, fabric C

*Finishing*
- Nine 3" strips, border 1 fabric
- Ten $5^1/2$" strips, border 2 fabric
- Ten $2^1/2$" strips, binding fabric

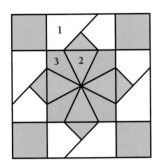

**Star Flower
Block – Fabrics**

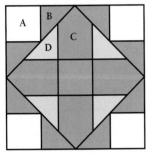

**Cross Within a Cross
Block – Fabrics**

## Layout 7 – Stars and Flowers

Approximate Size: 61" x 71"
Blocks Used: 15 Star Flower Blocks
(page 46) and 15 Cross Within a Cross
Blocks (page 32)

### Materials
*Star Flower Blocks*
- $2^3/8$ yds fabric 1
- $3/4$ yd fabric 2
- $1^1/8$ yds fabric 3

*Cross Within a Cross Blocks*
- $1/2$ yd fabric 1
- $3/4$ yd fabric 2
- $5/8$ yd fabric 3
- $3/8$ yd fabric 4

*Finishing*
- $1/2$ yd border 1 fabric
- $1^1/8$ yds border 2 fabric
- $5/8$ yd binding fabric
- $3^1/2$ yds backing fabric

### Suggested Cutting
*Note: Cut fabric into strips, then cut strips
as you piece referring to How to Make a
Foundation-Pieced Block, pages 3 to 5.*

*Star Flower Blocks*
- 20 – $3^1/4$" strips, fabric 1
- Five $3^1/4$" strips, fabric 1
- Two $2^1/2$" strips, fabric 2
- Six 3" strips, fabric 2
- Five 3" strips, fabric 3
- Seven 3" strips, fabric 3

*Cross Within a Cross Blocks*
- Five 3" strips, fabric A
- Seven $3^1/2$" strips, fabric B
- Seven 3" strips, fabric C
- Three $3^1/2$" strips, fabric D

*Finishing*
- Seven 2" strips, border 1 fabric
- Eight $4^1/2$" strips, border 2 fabric
- Eight $2^1/2$" strips, binding fabric

## Layout 8 – Ducks and Geese

Approximate Size: 65½" x 75½"
Blocks Used: 15 Duck Paddle Blocks
(page 30) and 15 Goose Tracks Blocks
(page 36)

**Materials**

*Duck Paddle Blocks*
- ¾ yd fabric 1
- ⅝ yd fabric 2
- ½ yd fabric 3
- ⅜ yd fabric 4
- ⅝ yd fabric 5

*Goose Tracks Blocks*
- 1 yd fabric A
- ½ yd fabric B
- ½ yd fabric C
- ⅜ yd fabric D
- ⅜ yd fabric E
- ⅛ yd fabric F

*Finishing*
- ½ yd border 1 fabric
- ½ yd border 2 fabric
- 1⅛ yds border 3 fabric
- ⅝ yd binding fabric
- 3¾ yds backing fabric

**Suggested Cutting**

*Note: Cut fabric into strips, then cut strips
as you piece referring to How to Make a
Foundation-Pieced Block, pages 3 to 5.*

*Duck Paddle Blocks*
- Eight 2½" strips, fabric 1
- Ten 2" strips, fabric 2
- One 2½" strips, fabric 3
- Four 3" strips, fabric 4
- Seven 2½" strips, fabric 5

*Goose Tracks Blocks*
- Eight 2½" strips, fabric A
- Six 2" strips, fabric A
- Nine 1½" strips, fabric B
- 11 – 1½" strips, fabric C
- Three 3" strips, fabric D
- Four 2½" strips, fabric E
- One 2½" strip, fabric F

*Finishing*
- Six 2¾" strips, border 1 fabric
- Seven 2" strips, border 2 fabric
- Eight 4½" strips, border 3 fabric
- Eight 2½" strips, binding fabric

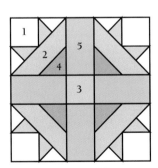

**Duck Paddle
Block – Fabrics**

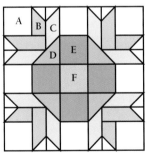

**Goose Tracks
Block – Fabrics**

# Putting the Quilt Top Together

Lay out blocks in desired arrangement. Sew quilt blocks together in rows; press seams for rows in alternate directions. Sew rows together, matching seams.

To add borders, measure quilt top lengthwise; cut two border strips to that length and sew to sides of quilt. Measure quilt top crosswise, including borders just added; cut two border strips to that length. Sew to top and bottom edges of quilt top. Repeat for any additional borders.

## Layering the Quilt

There are many types of batting on the market. Use batting that is suitable for the use of your quilt. If making a wall hanging, choose a thin cotton or polyester batting. If making a bed quilt, you may want a low-loft polyester batting for a little more thickness. Check the label to see the quilting requirements and follow those guidelines.

Use 100-percent cotton fabric for the backing of your quilt. For quilts wider than the 40"- to 44"-wide fabric, you will have to piece your backing unless you use the 90"- to 106"- wide fabrics that are currently available.

Cut backing and batting about 1" to 2" larger on all sides than the quilt top. Place backing wrong side up, then smooth out batting on top. Center quilt top right side up on batting.

Baste layers together using one of the following techniques:

**Fusible iron-on batting** – The new Fusible Batting™ by June Tailor and Gold-Fuse by Mountain Mist® are a wonderful new way to hold the quilt layers together without using other time-consuming methods of basting.

**Thread basting** – Baste with long stitches, starting in center and sewing toward edges in a number of diagonal lines.

**Safety pin basting** – Pin through all layers at once, starting from center and working toward edges. Place pins no more than 4" apart, thinking of your quilt plan as you work to make certain pins avoid prospective quilting lines.

**Quilt gun basting** – Use the handy trigger tool (found in quilt and fabric stores) that pushes nylon tags through all layers of the quilt. Start in center and work randomly toward outside edges. Place tags about 4" apart. You can sew right over the tags and then easily remove them by cutting off with a pair of scissors.

**Spray or heat-set basting** – Use one of the spray adhesives currently on the market, following manufacturer's directions.

## Quilting

If you have never used a sewing machine for quilting, you might want to read more about the technique. *Learn to Machine Quilt in Just One Weekend* (ASN #4186), by Marti Michell, is an excellent introduction to machine quilting. This book is available at your local quilt or fabric store, or write the publisher for a list of sources.

You do not need a special machine for quilting. Just make sure your machine is oiled and in good working condition. An even-feed foot is a good investment if you are going to machine quilt, since it is designed to feed the top and bottom layers of the quilt through the machine evenly. Use fine transparent nylon thread in the top and regular sewing thread in the bobbin.

To quilt in the ditch of a seam (this is actually stitching in the space between two pieces of fabric that have been sewn together), use your fingers to pull blocks or pieces apart slightly and machine-stitch right between the two pieces. Try to keep stitching to the side of the seam that does not have the bulk of the seam allowance under it. When you have finished stitching, the quilting will be practically hidden in the seam.

Free-form machine quilting is done with a darning foot and the feed dogs down on your sewing machine. It can be used to quilt around a design or to quilt a motif. Free-form machine quilting takes practice to master because you are controlling the movement of the quilt under the needle, rather than the machine moving the quilt. With free-form machine quilting, you can quilt in any direction: up and down, side to side and even in circles, without pivoting the quilt around the needle.

## Attaching the Binding

Trim backing and batting even with quilt top. Cut enough 2½"-wide strips to go around all four sides of quilt, plus 6". Join strips end to end with diagonal seams; trim corners, **Fig 32**.

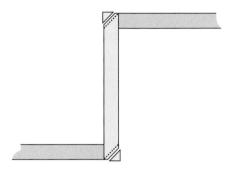

**Fig 32**

Press seams open. Cut one end of strip at a 45-degree angle, then press under ¼", **Fig 33**.

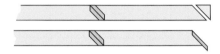

**Fig 33**

Press entire strip in half lengthwise, wrong sides together, **Fig 34**.

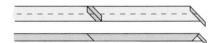

**Fig 34**

On right side of quilt, position binding in middle of one side, aligning raw edges. Sew binding to quilt using ¼" seam, beginning about an inch below folded end of binding, **Fig 35**.

**Fig 35**

At corner, stop ¼" from edge of quilt and backstitch. Fold binding away from quilt at a 45-degree angle. Fold binding back on itself so fold is on quilt edge and raw edges are aligned with adjacent side of quilt, **Fig 36**. Begin sewing at quilt edge.

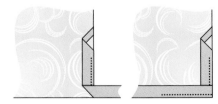

**Fig 36**

Continue in the same manner around remaining sides of quilt. To finish, stop about two inches away from starting point. Trim excess binding, then tuck inside folded end, **Fig 37**. Finish line of stitching.

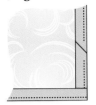

**Fig 37**

Fold binding to back of quilt so seam line is covered; blindstitch in place.

**The Finishing Touch**

After your quilt is finished, always sign and date it. A label can be cross-stitched, embroidered or even written with a permanent marking pen. To make decorative labels in a hurry, *Iron-on Transfers for Quilt Labels* (ASN #4188) and *Foundation-Pieced Quilt Labels* (ASN

#4196) provide many patterns for fun and unique quilt labels. Hand-stitch to back of quilt.

# 1 - Country Husband

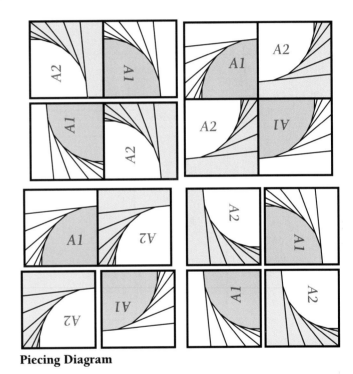

**Piecing Diagram**

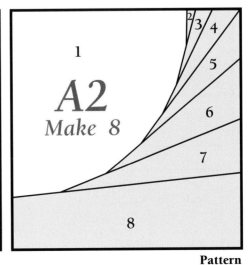

**Pattern**

# 2 - Desert Rose

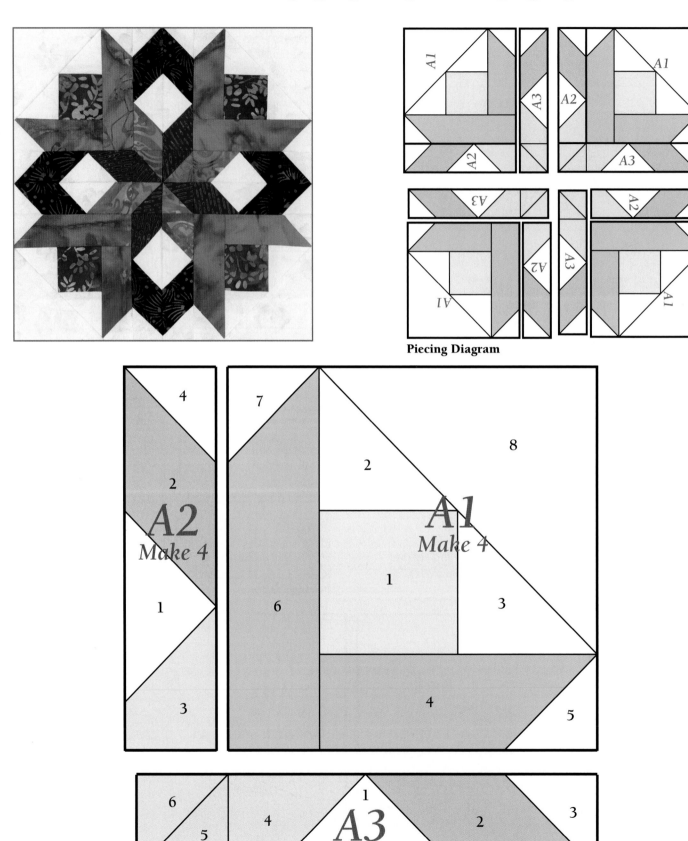

**Piecing Diagram**

**Pattern**

# 3 - Carpenter's Wheel

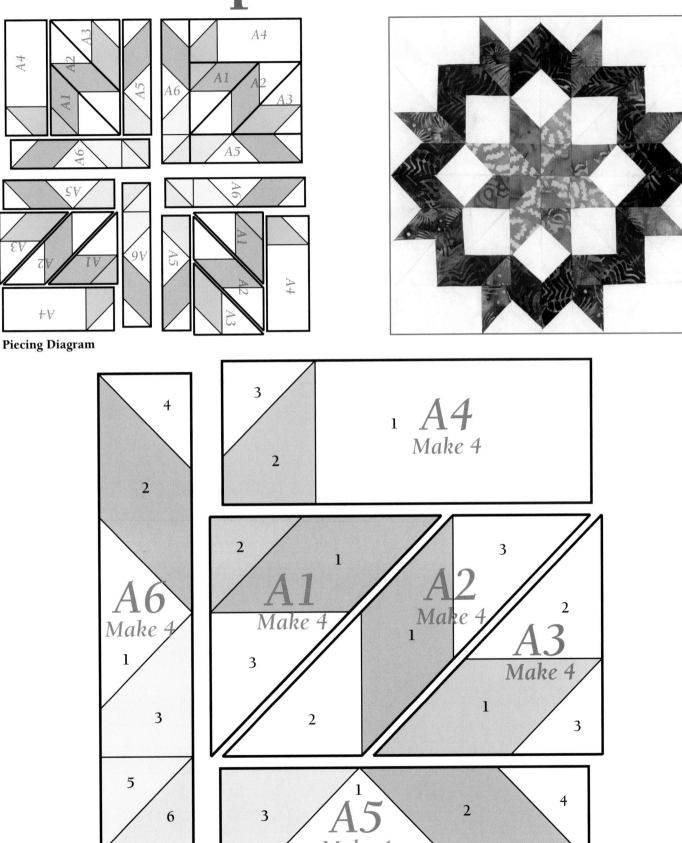

**Piecing Diagram**

A4 — Make 4
A6 — Make 4
A1 — Make 4
A2 — Make 4
A3 — Make 4
A5 — Make 4

**Pattern**

# 4 - Children of Israel

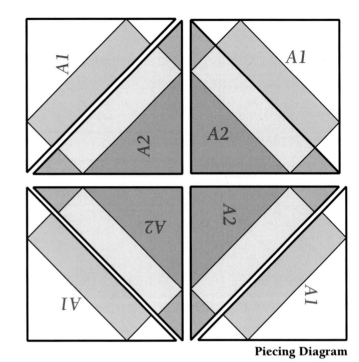

**Piecing Diagram**

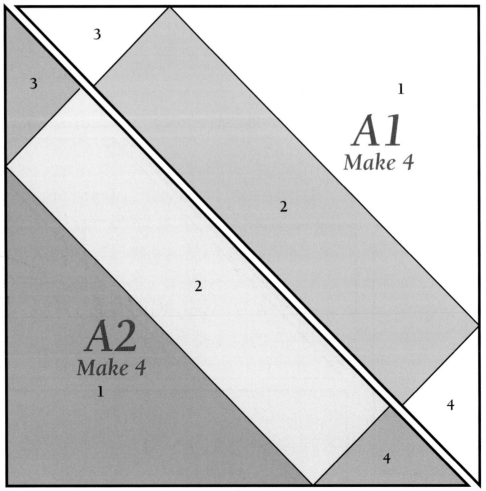

**Pattern**

# 5 - Fly Foot

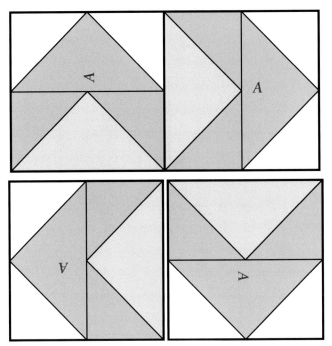

**Piecing Diagram**

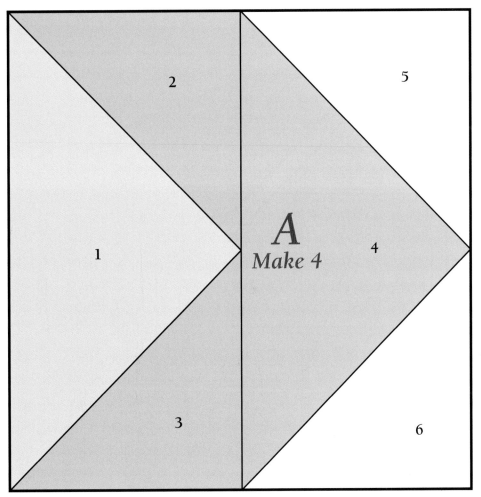

A
Make 4

**Pattern**

# 6 - Exploding Star

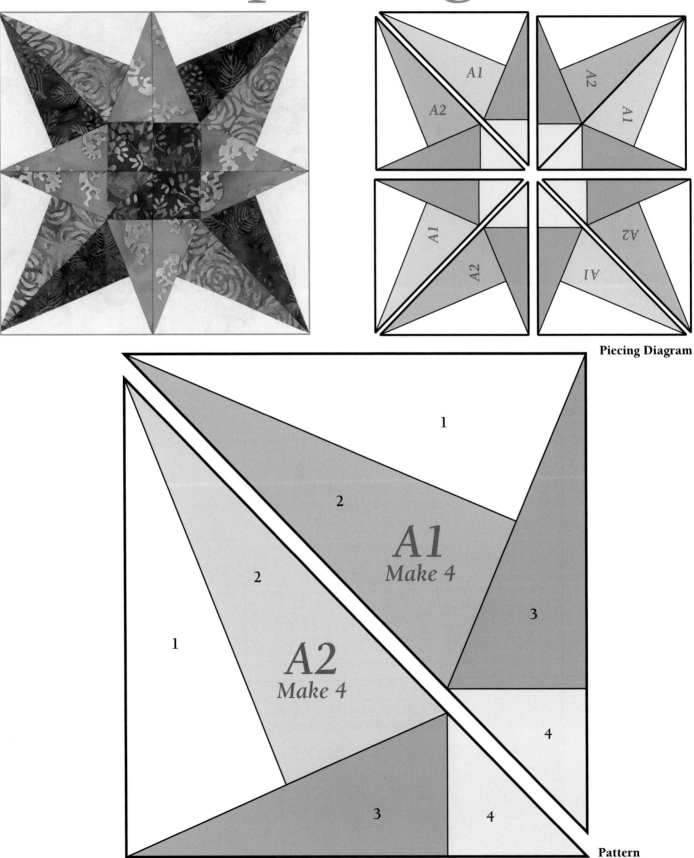

**Piecing Diagram**

A1 Make 4

A2 Make 4

**Pattern**

# 7 - Snow Crystals

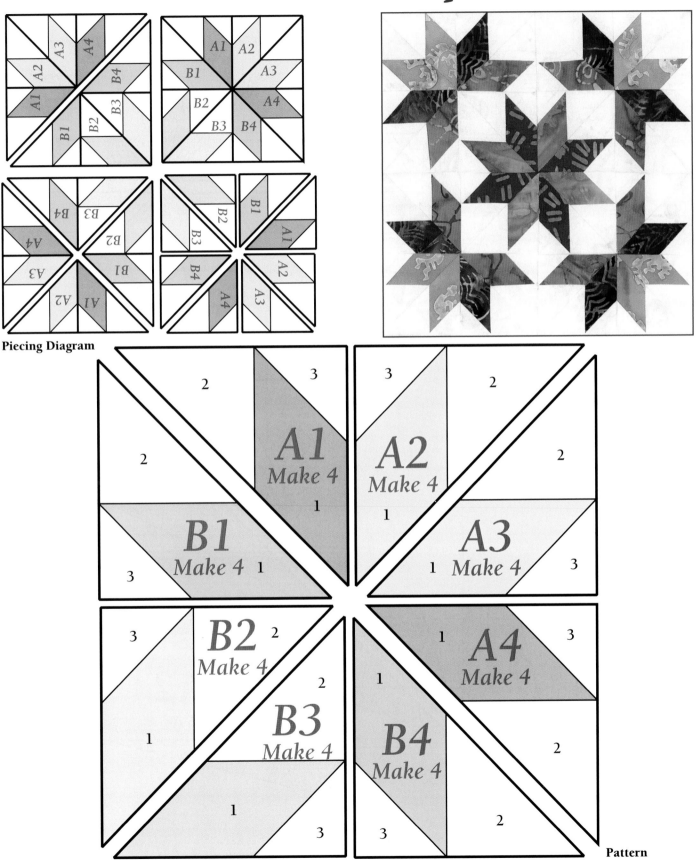

**Piecing Diagram**

**Pattern**

# 8 - Palm Leaves

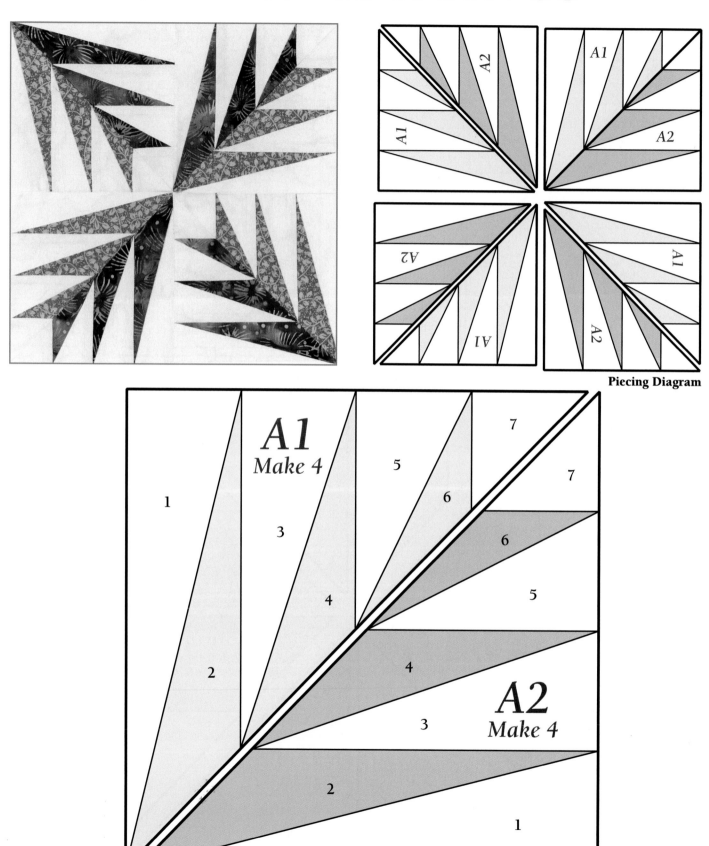

**Piecing Diagram**

A1
Make 4

A2
Make 4

**Pattern**

# 9 - Tail of Benjamin's Kite

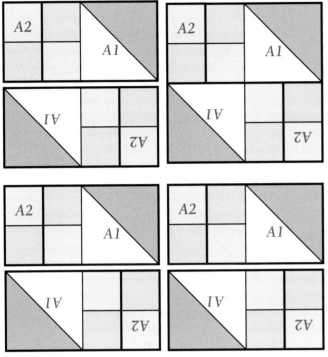

**Piecing Diagram**

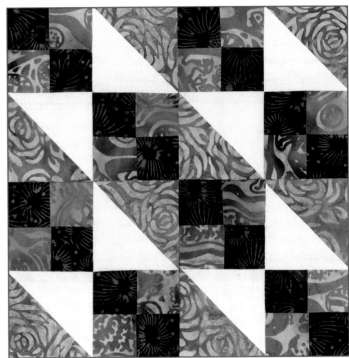

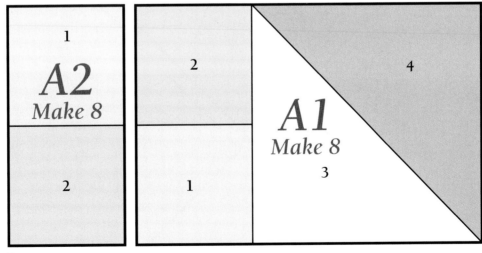

**Pattern**

# 10 - Four-Point

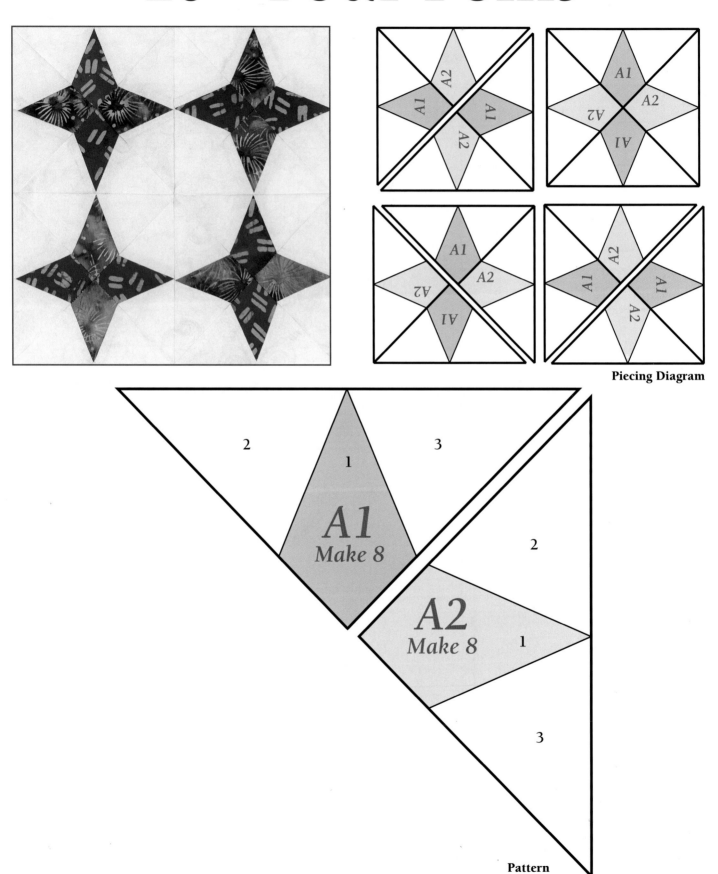

**Piecing Diagram**

A1
Make 8

A2
Make 8

**Pattern**

# 11 - Oh Susannah

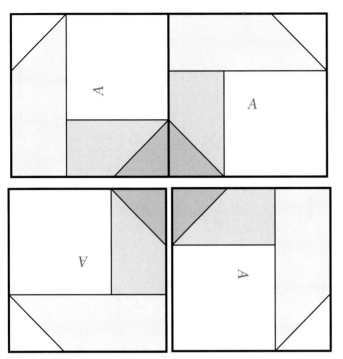

**Piecing Diagram**

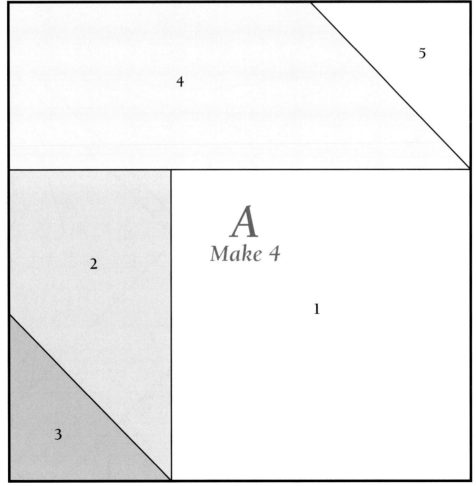

*A*
*Make 4*

**Pattern**

# 12 - Orange Peel

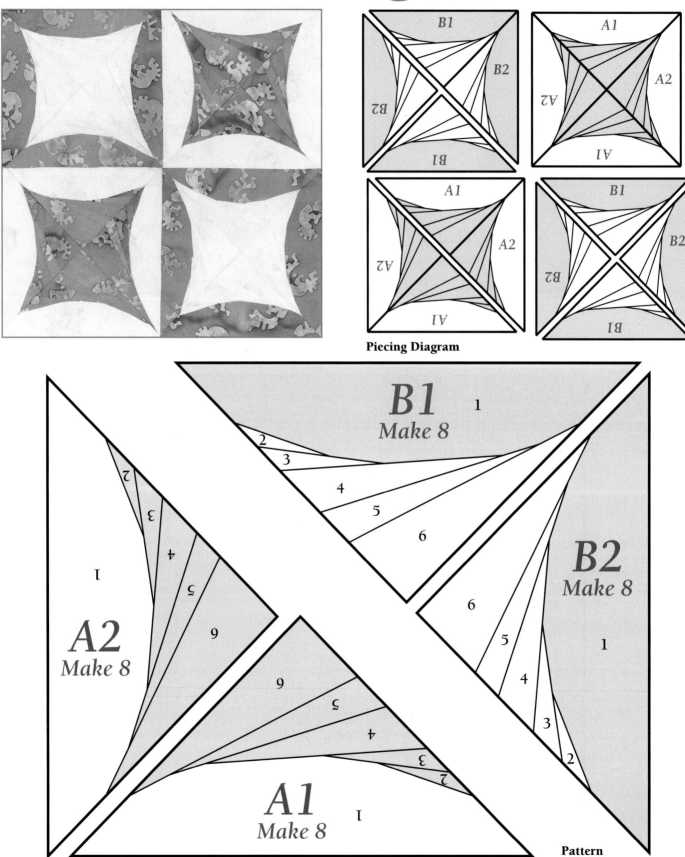

**Piecing Diagram**

B1
Make 8

B2
Make 8

A2
Make 8

A1
Make 8

**Pattern**

# 13 - Swing in the Center

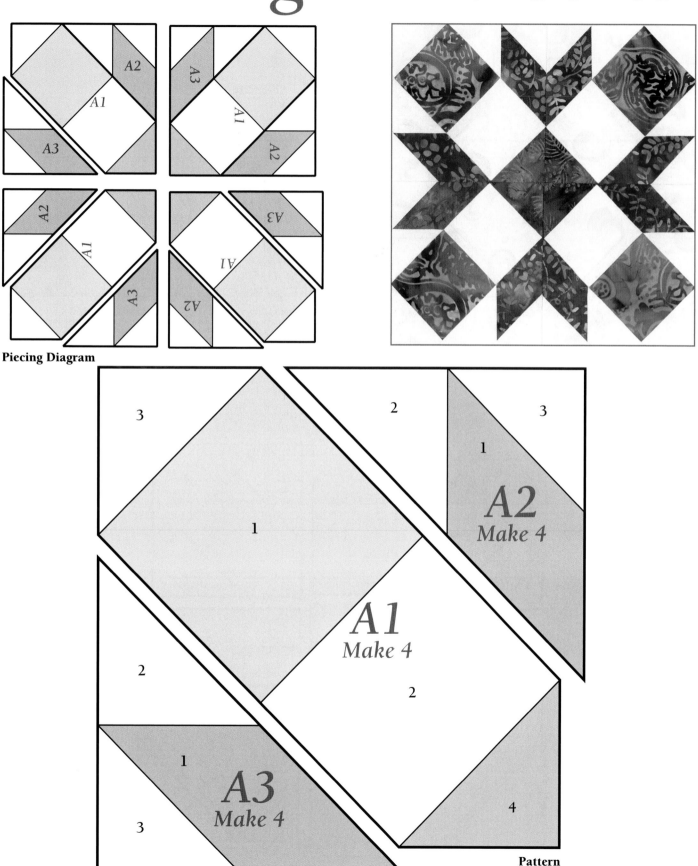

**Piecing Diagram**

**A2**
Make 4

**A1**
Make 4

**A3**
Make 4

**Pattern**

# 14 - Star of Bethlehem

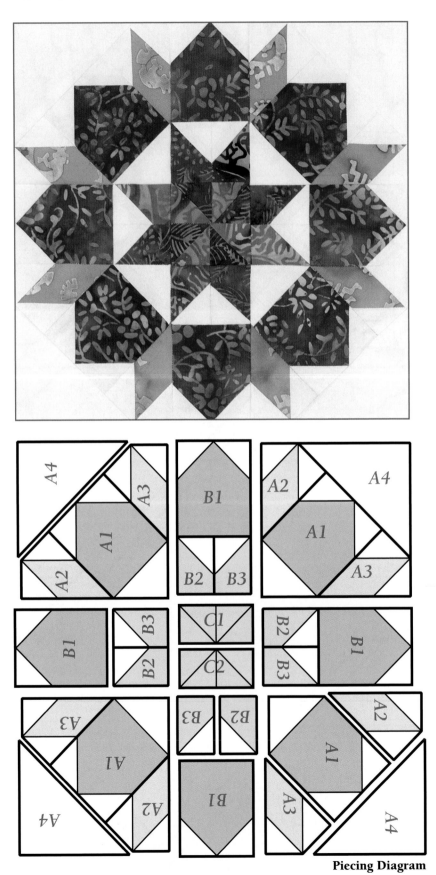

**Piecing Diagram**

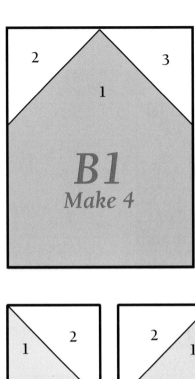

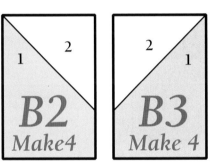

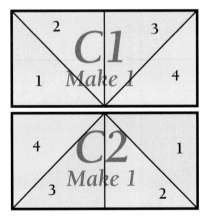

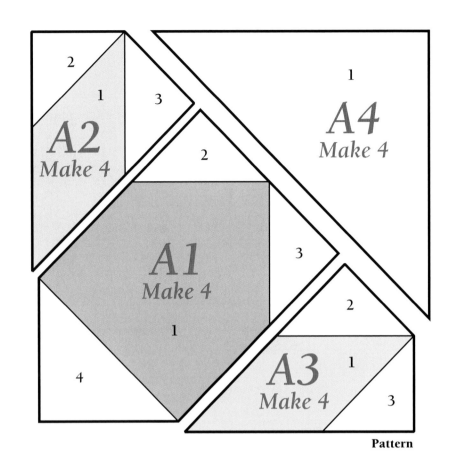

**Pattern**

# 15 - Duck Paddle

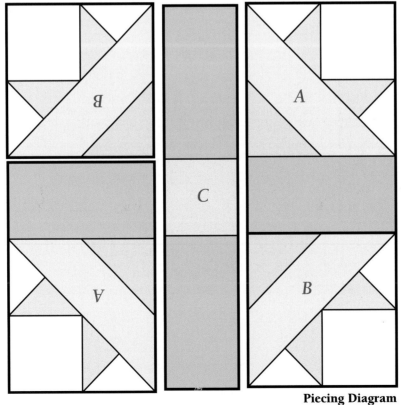

**Piecing Diagram**

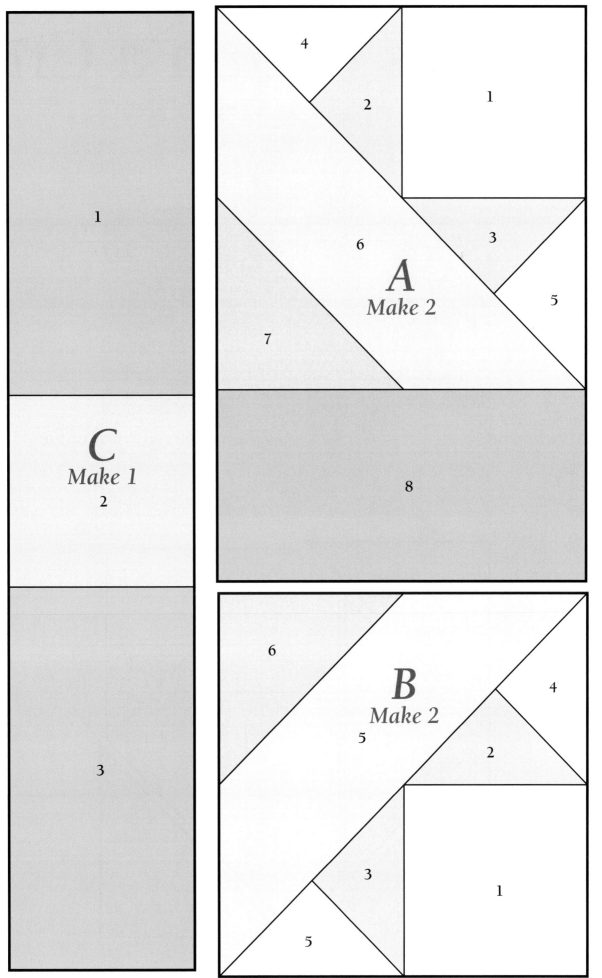

# 16 - Cross Within a Cross

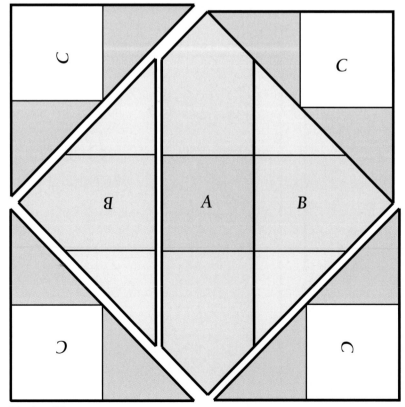

**Piecing Diagram**

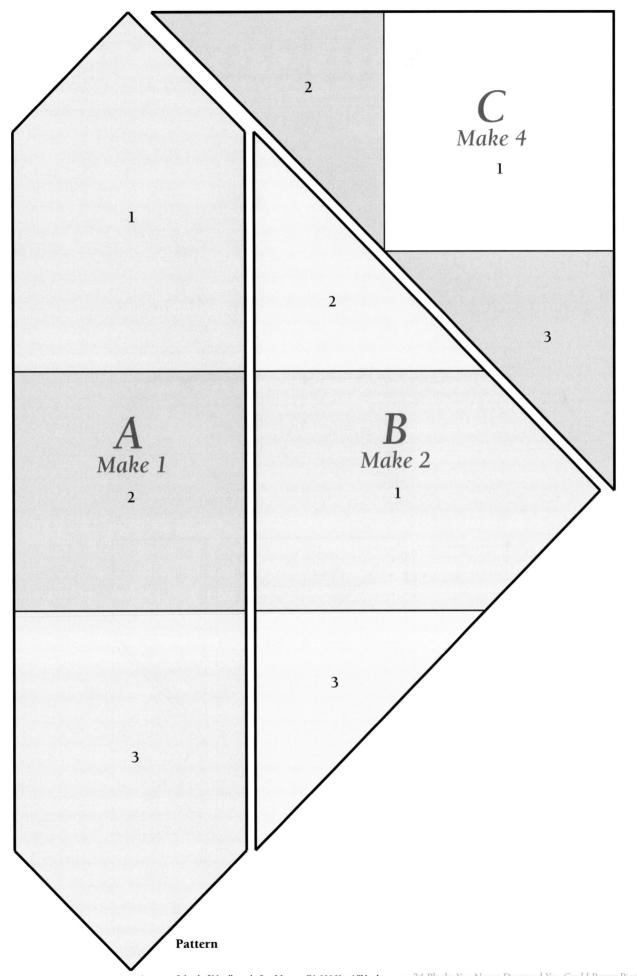

A
*Make 1*

1

2

3

B
*Make 2*

2

1

3

C
*Make 4*

1

2

3

**Pattern**

# 17 - Twinkling Star

**Piecing Diagram**

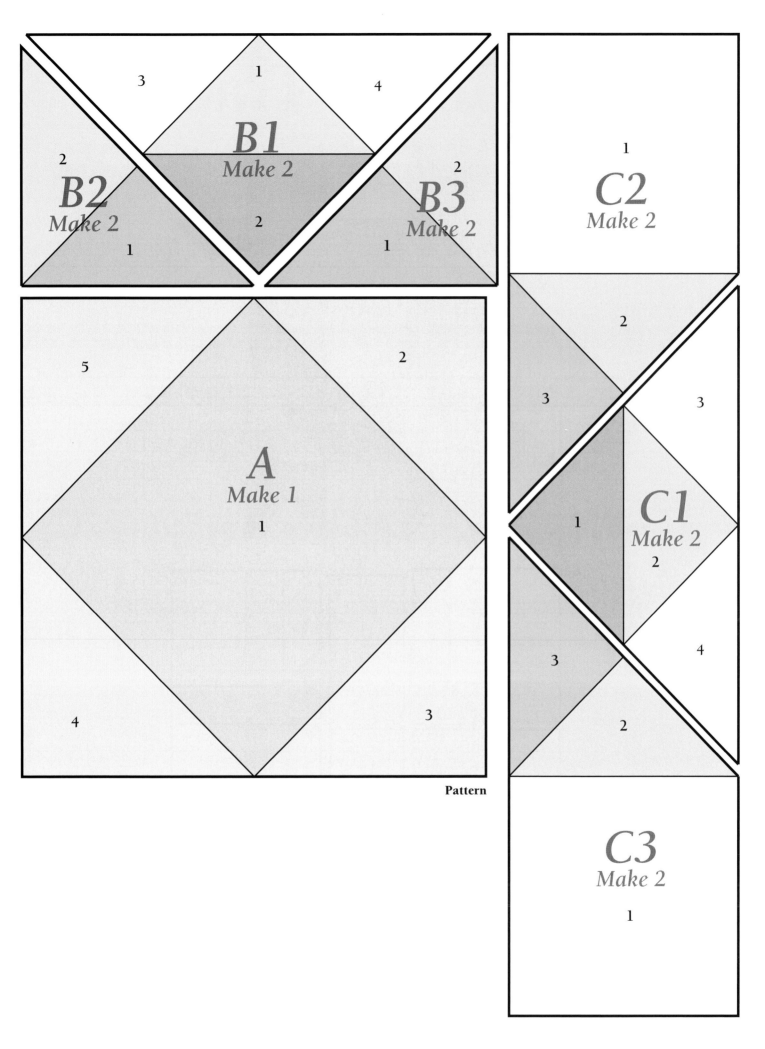

**Pattern**

# 18 - Goose Tracks

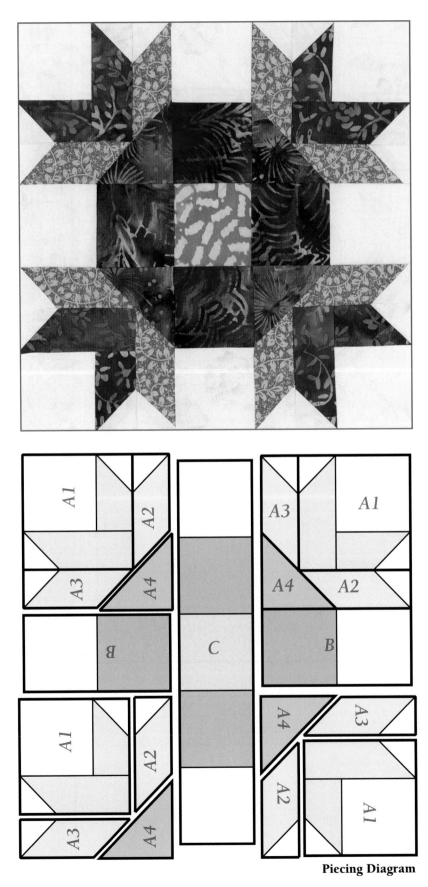

**Piecing Diagram**

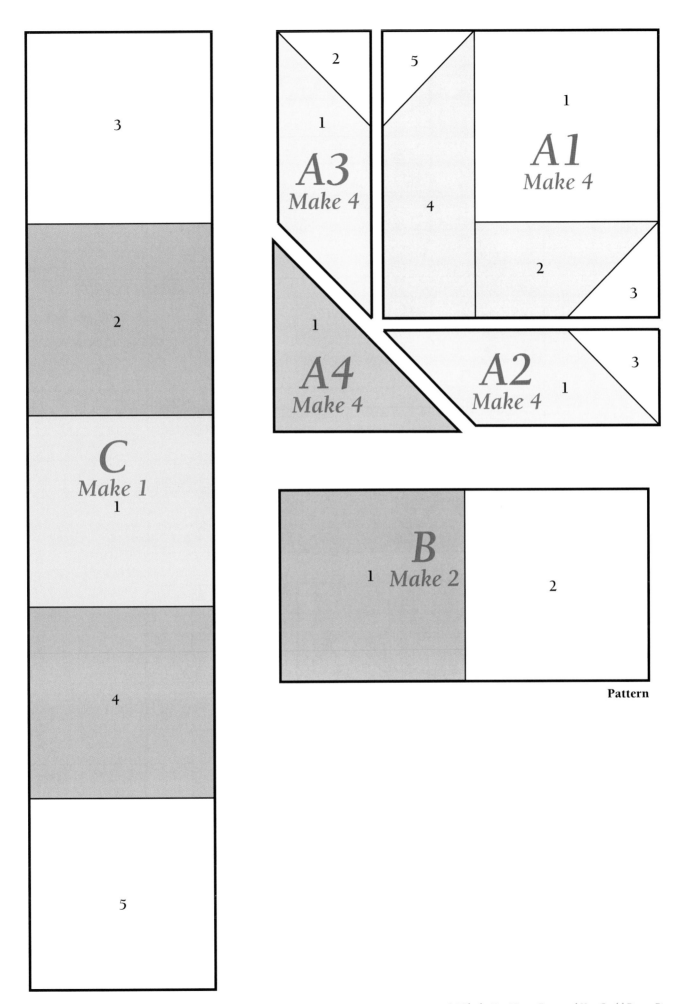

# 19 - Crow Foot

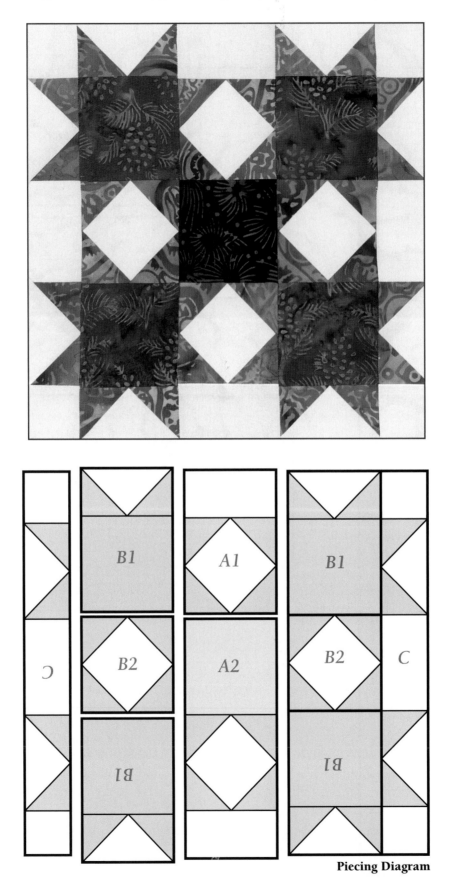

**Piecing Diagram**

*24 Blocks You Never Dreamed You Could Paper Piece* • American School of Needlework, San Marcos, CA 92069 • ASNpub.com

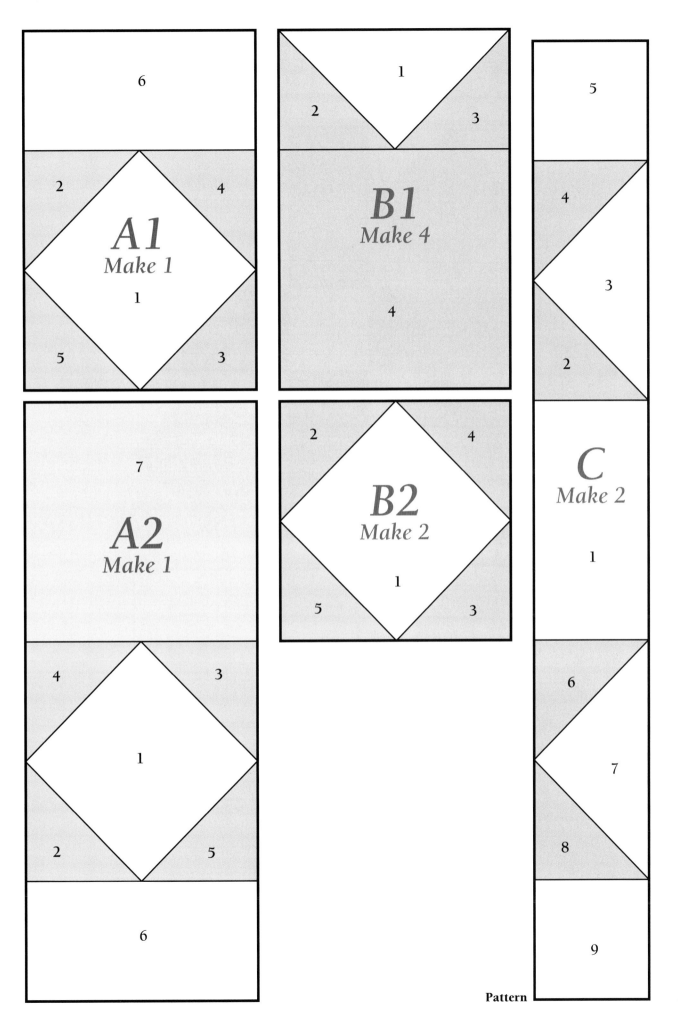

A1
Make 1

6

2    4

A1
Make 1

1

5    3

A2
Make 1

7

4    3

1

2    5

6

B1
Make 4

1

2    3

4

B2
Make 2

2    4

B2
Make 2

1

5    3

C
Make 2

5

4

3

2

1

6

7

8

9

# 20 - Garden of Eden

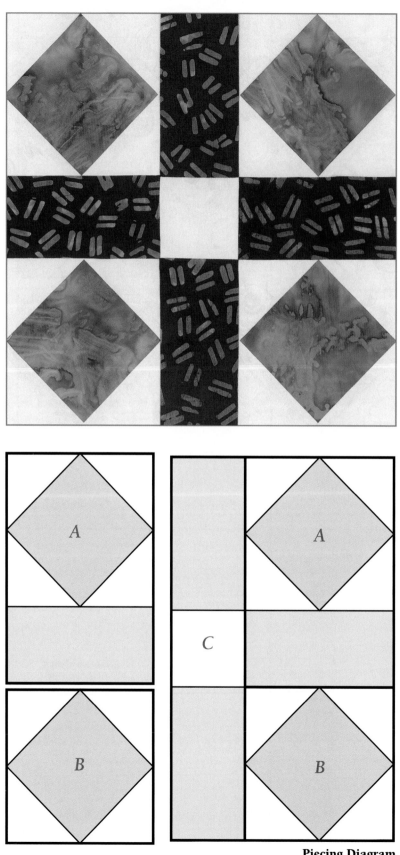

**Piecing Diagram**

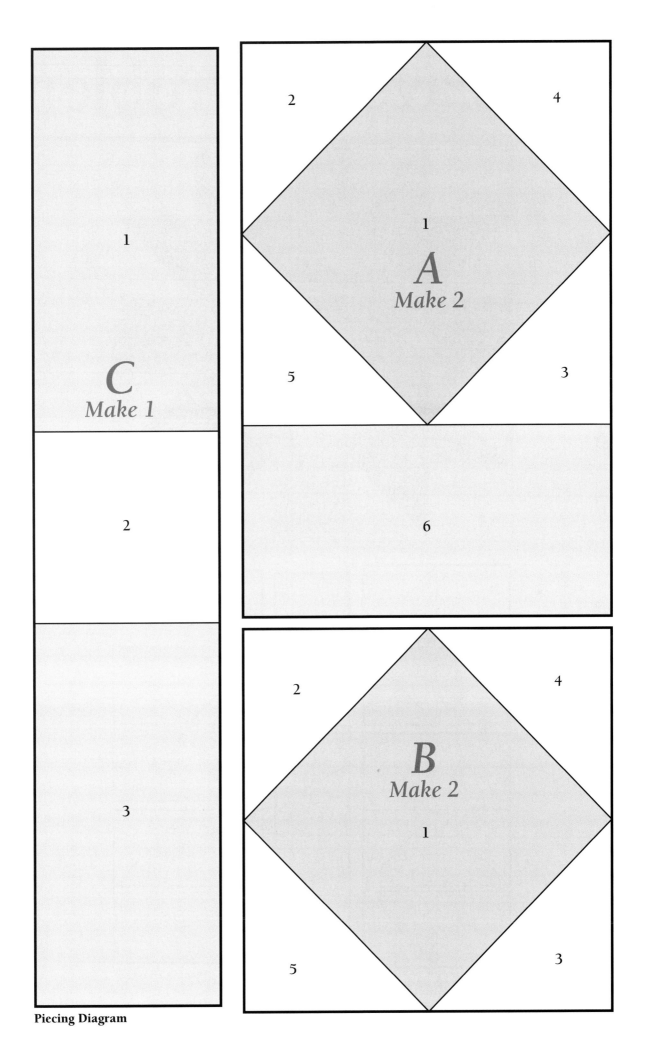

**Piecing Diagram**

41

# 21 - Heavenly Problems

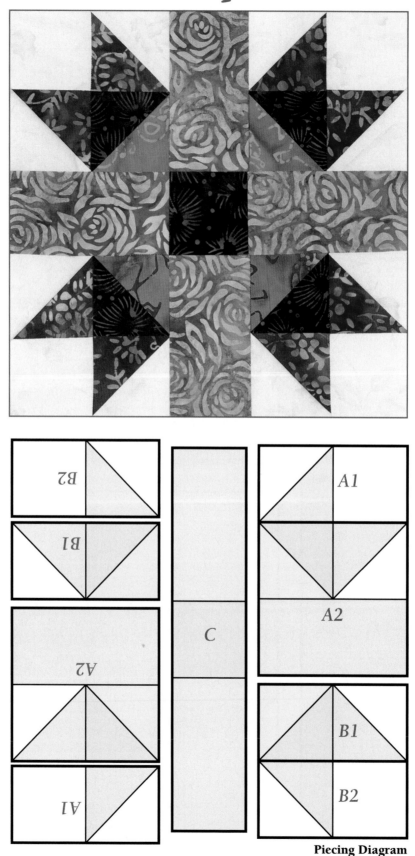

**Piecing Diagram**

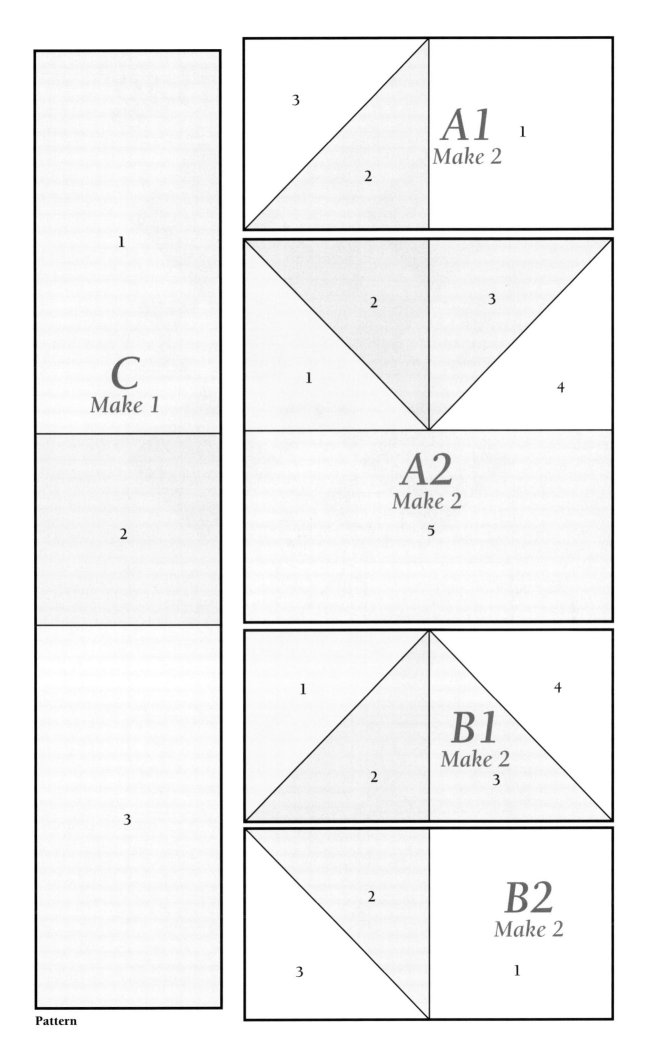

**Pattern**

43

# 22 - Scrap Bag

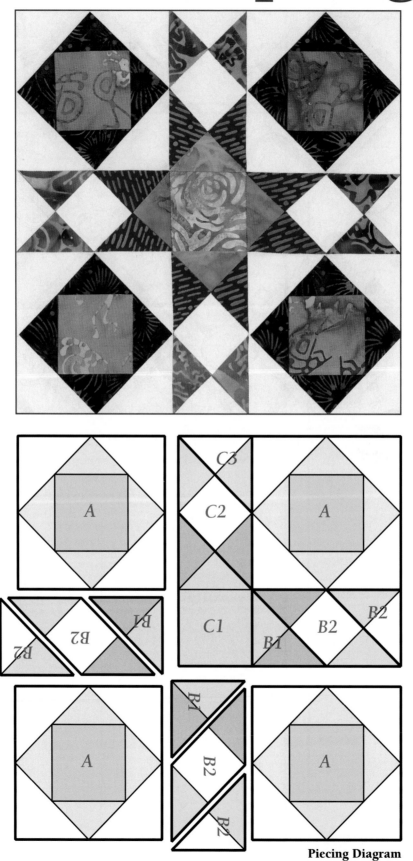

**Piecing Diagram**

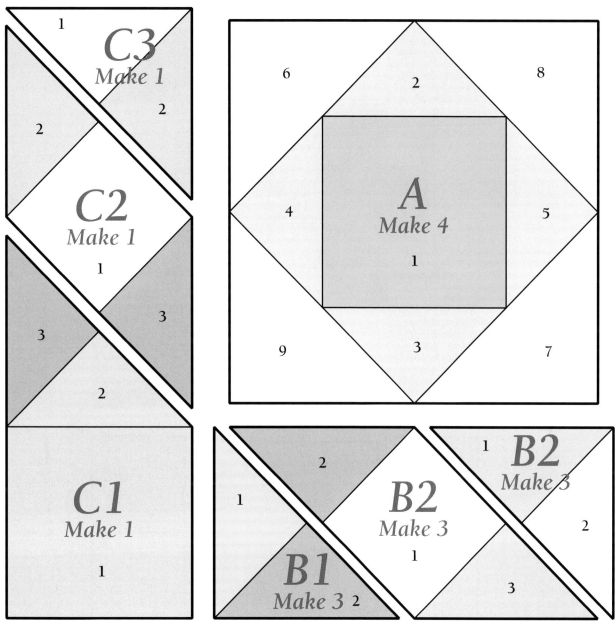

**C3**
*Make 1*

1

2

2

**C2**
*Make 1*

1

3

3

2

**C1**
*Make 1*

1

**A**
*Make 4*

6

2

8

4

5

1

9

3

7

**B2**
*Make 3*

1

2

**B2**
*Make 3*

2

1

1

3

**B1**
*Make 3*

1

2

Pattern

# 23 - Star Flower

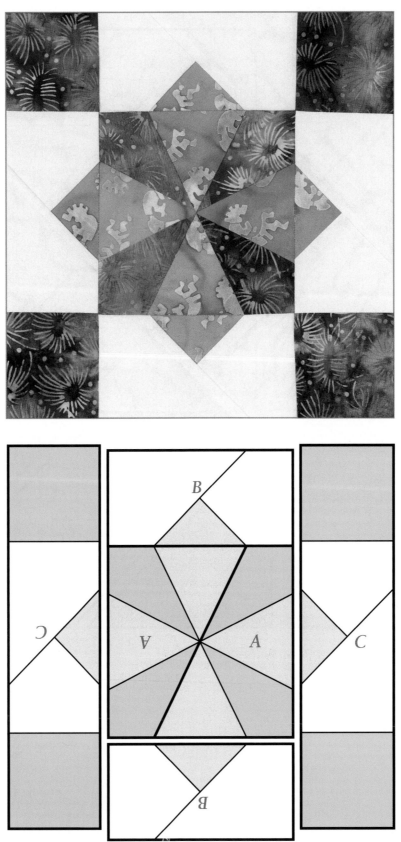

**Piecing Diagram**

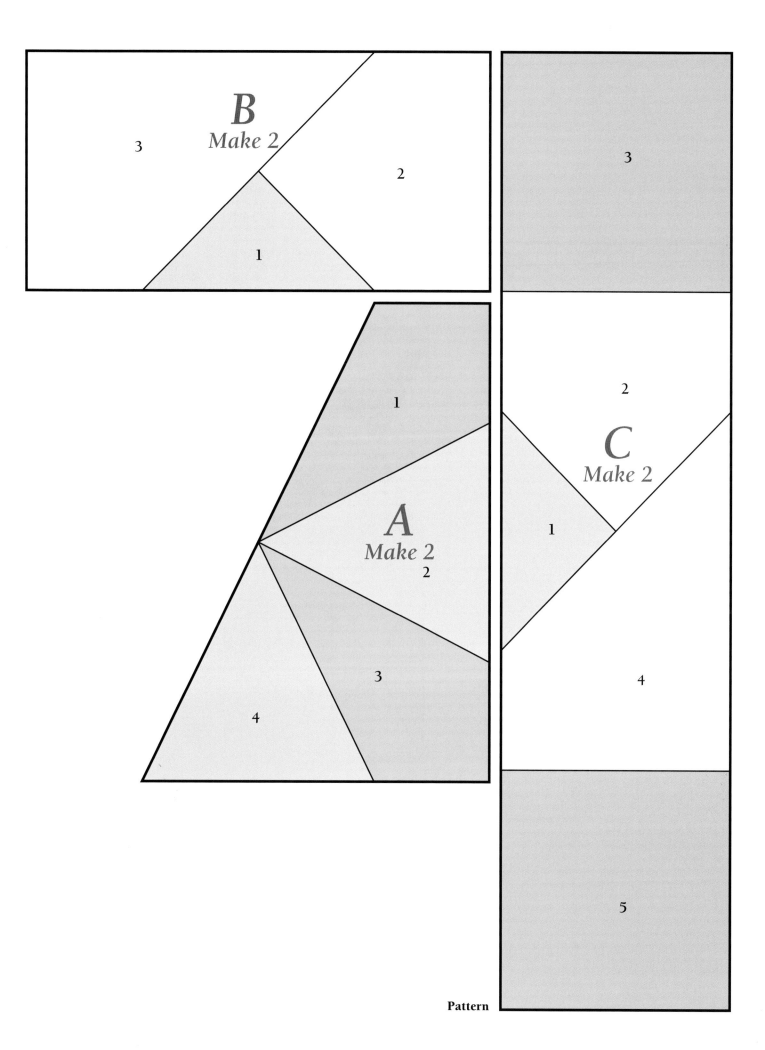

B
*Make 2*

3

2

1

A
*Make 2*

1

2

3

4

C
*Make 2*

2

1

3

4

5

**Pattern**

# 24 - Windmill Star

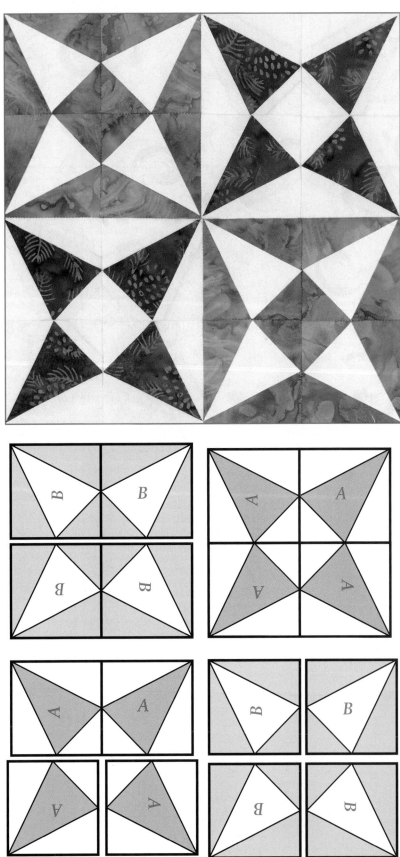

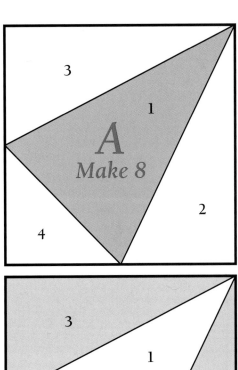

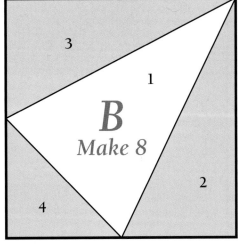

**Pattern**

**Piecing Diagram**